Sports

Basketball

by Nick Rebman

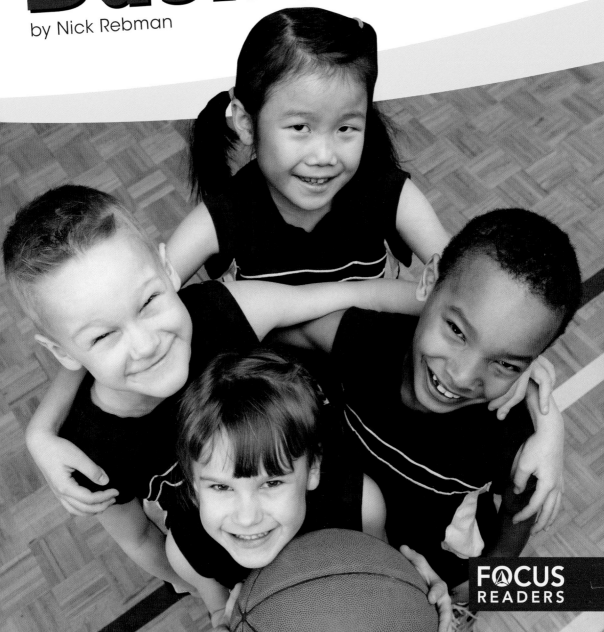

FOCUS
READERS

www.focusreaders.com

Focus Readers is distributed by North Star Editions:
sales@northstareditions.com | 888-417-0195

Produced for Focus Readers by Red Line Editorial.

Photographs ©: FatCamera/iStockphoto, cover, 1, 11, 15; Cosmin Iftode/Dreamstime, 4; xavierarnau/iStockphoto, 7; Elizaveta Galitckaia/Shutterstock Images, 9 (foreground), 16 (top right); Oleg Mikhaylov/Shutterstock Images, 9 (background); Sergey Novikov/Shutterstock Images, 13, 16 (bottom left); Joseph Sohm/Shutterstock Images, 16 (top left); Brocreative/Shutterstock Images, 16 (bottom right)

ISBN
978-1-63517-916-3 (hardcover)
978-1-64185-018-6 (paperback)
978-1-64185-220-3 (ebook pdf)
978-1-64185-119-0 (hosted ebook)

Library of Congress Control Number: 2018931982

Printed in the United States of America
Mankato, MN
May, 2018

About the Author

Nick Rebman enjoys reading, drawing, and traveling to places where he doesn't speak the language. He lives in Minnesota.

Table of Contents

Basketball

Basketball is fun.

Two teams play.

They play on a **court**.

Players need a **hoop**.

Players need a ball.

Players need **shoes**.

Safety

Players can wear

mouth guards.

Mouth guards keep

teeth safe.

mouth guard

How to Play

Players cannot run with
the ball.
Players must bounce
the ball.
This is called dribbling.

A player shoots the ball.

The ball goes into the hoop.

The team gets two points.

One team scores

more points.

This team wins.

The players are happy.

Glossary

court

mouth guards

hoop

shoes

Index